SOUTH EAST AFRICA

SOUTH EAST AFRICA
ZIMBABWE, ZAMBIA, MALAWI, MADAGASCAR, MAURITIUS, AND RÉUNION

BY L. B. TAYLOR, JR.

FRANKLIN WATTS

New York | London | Toronto | Sydney | 1981

A FIRST BOOK

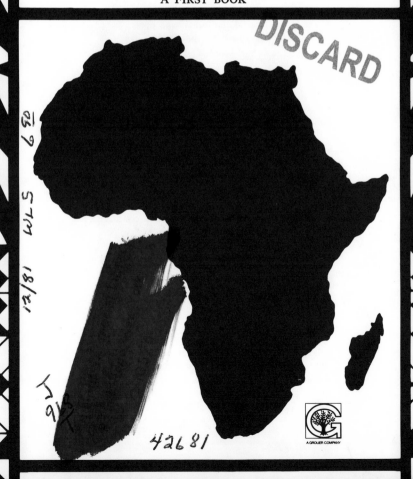

Cover design by Jackie Schuman

Photographs courtesy of:
Bruce Coleman, Inc. (Keith Gunnar): p. 8;
Bruce Coleman Inc. (Mark Boulton): p. 27;
Photo Researchers (Diane Rawson): p. 13;
Photo Researchers (Frederick Ayer): pp. 42, 47, 50;
World Health Organization: p. 21;
Sygma (Peter Marlow): p. 34;
United Press International: p. 37;
FAO: p. 53.

Maps courtesy of Vantage Art, Inc.

Library of Congress Cataloging in Publication Data

Taylor, L   B
South East Africa.

(A First book)
Bibliography: p.
Includes index.
SUMMARY: An introduction to six countries
and islands of southeastern Africa.
1. Africa, Southern—Juvenile literature.
2. Islands of the Indian Ocean—Juvenile literature.
[1. Africa, Southern. 2. Islands of the Indian Ocean]
I. Title.
DT729.5.T39   968   80-24753
ISBN 0-531-04277-4

CONTENTS

SOUTH EAST AFRICA

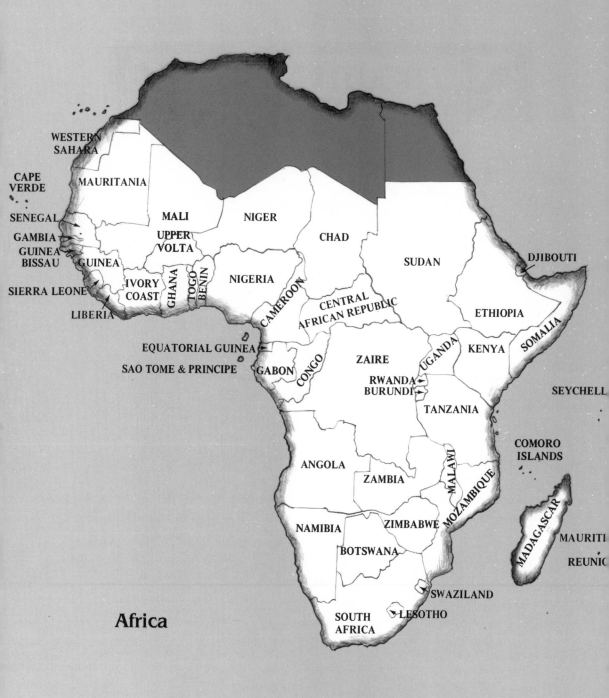

Africa

NATIONS IN THE NEWS

For dozens of centuries very little was known about the region of south-central Africa that includes the bordering nations of Zimbabwe, Zambia, and Malawi. It was cloaked in mystery to all but the Africans who lived there. The same was true, to a lesser extent, of three major islands off the eastern coast of Africa: the giant-sized Madagascar, and the smaller Mauritius and Réunion.

It was not until a little more than one hundred years ago, when Europeans began settling in great numbers in the lands now known as Zimbabwe, Zambia, and Malawi, that the outside world first learned what they were like. Reports then began coming out, telling of an area rich in gold, copper, and other natural resources, and with great herds of ivory-tusked elephants and a variety of other animals that roamed freely over high grassy plains.

More had been known about the islands than the mainland, because Europeans and Indonesians had landed there centuries earlier. They were easier to reach than the landlocked countries which were hundreds of miles from the coast. However, it was not until the late 1800s that these islands, too, began to gain widespread attention.

Today, though, many of these lands are often in the news. This was particularly true of Zimbabwe as it struggled for independence during the last decade. In fact, in this part of Africa, and on the islands, the fight for freedom and individual rights has been long, bitter, and at times bloody.

As white settlers moved in—the British into Zimbabwe, Zambia, and Malawi; the British and French onto Madagascar; and the French onto Mauritius and Réunion—their paths were trailblazed by some famous adventurers. These included the noted missionary-explorer, Dr. David Livingstone, and the pioneering businessman, Cecil Rhodes.

Some people sought quick wealth not only from the riches in the soil, but also from the people of the land. Slavery still was a going trade at the time. The continuing call for more slaves to work the plantations in the Americas sent merciless traders deeper into the African countryside, and into the interiors of the islands, in search of more bodies.

These European newcomers often ruled with an iron hand. They took over the land as they went, even though they made up only a small percentage of the total population, sometimes less than 5 percent.

The white settlers were better organized, and were equipped with newer and more powerful weapons than were the Africans. They could quickly put an end to any uprising.

The native Africans were stripped of most of their freedom and lost much of the land on which their tribal families had lived for centuries.

Such foreign control lasted for nearly one hundred years. Not all of it was bad. The Europeans introduced many modern ways. Using native labor, they built roads and railways. They improved farming and fishing methods. They used new means to mine such natural resources as copper and chromium.

Still, it was the black Africans' homeland, and they would never be happy until they could claim it for themselves and rule their own lives.

This dream finally came true for many African nations in the 1960s when they gained their independence as colonial days ended. Zambia, Malawi, Madagascar, and Mauritius were among these lands. Réunion still is governed as an overseas department of France.

In Zimbabwe, the white settlers stayed in charge. They refused an order from England to turn the country back to rule by its native people. So the conflict in this torn country went on through the 1970s.

Not only was there unrest in Zimbabwe, but it also affected neighboring nations. Zambians, trying to help their black friends, were caught up in the fight. It continued into the early 1980s. Today, although a truce has been declared and Africans now rule their own country, the situation still is tense.

For untold centuries, Zimbabwe, Zambia, Malawi, Madagascar, Mauritius, and Réunion lay far off the beaten track, sealed in mystery. Now these countries and islands are a story that is as fresh and as fascinating as today's newspaper.

2
COMMON HIGH GROUND

The bordering countries of Zimbabwe, Zambia, and Malawi have much in common aside from their history and fight for independence. In climate, geography, culture, and other areas, these nations share a lot of similarities.

Roughly acorn-shaped, Zimbabwe is the southernmost of the three. It is connected to Zambia to the north by the famous Zambezi River. South Africa lies to the south; Botswana to the west; and Mozambique to the east. Zimbabwe is a rugged, beautiful country. Its area is 150,333 square miles (389,363 sq km)—about as big as the state of Montana.

Most of Zimbabwe is a high, rolling plateau, or "veld," 3,000 to 5,000 feet (915 to 1,525 m) above sea level. A high mountainous region of great beauty runs along the eastern border for more than 200 miles (323 km). The highest mountain, Inyangani, is about 8,500 feet (2,592 m) above sea level.

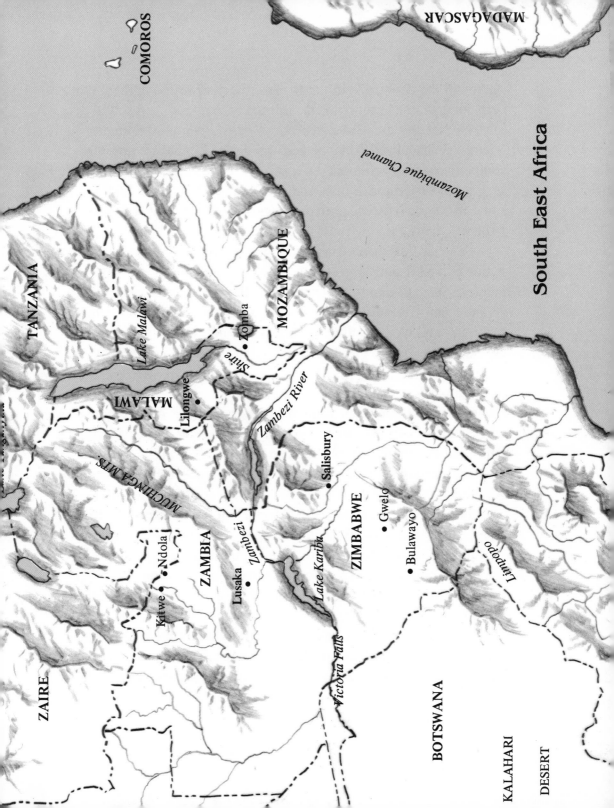

South East Africa

Although the country is in the tropics, the year-round climate is very comfortable because of the altitude.

One of the great scenic beauties of the world—the mighty Victoria Falls—lies on the northern border of Zimbabwe and the southern border of Zambia. It was named after Queen Victoria of England by the explorer and missionary Dr. David Livingstone in 1855. It is wider than Niagara Falls, and, at 355 feet (108 m), more than twice its height.

Salisbury, in the northeastern shoulder of Zimbabwe, is the nation's capital and largest city. It has a population estimated at more than 600,000. Bulawayo, in the southwestern sector, is the second largest city. It has a population of more than 350,000, and is a leading commercial and industrial center. Gwelo, in the middle of the country, is another important industrial site.

Zambia, directly north of Zimbabwe, is the largest of the three countries. It has an area of 290,586 square miles (752,618 sq km), and is slightly larger than the state of Texas. Named for the Zambezi River, Zambia is a butterfly-shaped country. The Zambezi, which extends down through the western part of Zambia, is one of four great rivers of Africa. The other three are the Nile, Niger, and Congo. The Zambezi flows for 1,700 miles (2,742 km) before it empties into the Indian Ocean.

Angola is on Zambia's western border. Tanzania lies to the north, Malawi and Mozambique to the east, and Zimbabwe to the south.

Most of Zambia is flat and covered with trees, bushes, grassy plains, and marshland. Like Zimbabwe, it lies on a high plateau, about 4,000 feet (1,220 m) above sea level. In the

[6]

northeast, the Muchinga Mountains rise to over 7,000 feet (2,135 m). Although the land is near the equator, because of the altitude the climate is warm, but not humid, and comfortable. It is much like that of southern California except there is less smog and more rain. The hot season is short, lasting only from September through November. During this period, midday temperatures range between 80° and 100° F (27° to 38° C). The rainy season lasts from November through April. From May through August, temperatures generally are about 20° F (10° C) cooler than in the hot season.

Zambia has eight provinces. Three are in the eastern, or right, wing of the "butterfly." They are the Luapula, Northern, and Eastern provinces. Luapula contains thousands of square miles of water, mud, and swamps, with much wildlife and vegetation. The Northern province borders on Lake Tanganyika, which is the world's seventh largest lake, 420 miles (677 km) long and containing 160 species of fish. Much of this land in this province is brown, dry, and not very scenic. The Eastern province is separated from the Northern one by the Muchinga Mountains, and this area features rolling hills and the highest points in Zambia.

The other five provinces lie in the country's western, or left, wing of the "butterfly." Few people live in the Northwestern province. The Western province is sandy in nature and borders on the Kalahari Desert. Valuable teak and mahogany forests also are located in this area.

The Southern province is dominated by two great water resources. One is Victoria Falls. The other is Lake Kariba, the largest man-made lake in the world. It is 175 miles long (282 km) and 20 miles (32 km) wide. North of this lake is the Cen-

tral province, which contains some of the best agricultural land in Zambia. And north of this is the Copperbelt province, which features heavy black soil and some of the richest and largest copper mines in the world.

Lusaka, in the south-central heart of Zambia, is the capital and largest city. It has a population of over 400,000. Kitwe, population 250,000, and Ndola, 220,000, are the second and third largest cities, and are important industrial sites. They are close together in the Copperbelt province in the north-central section.

Malawi, formerly known as Nyasaland, is a small, narrow, scenic country slightly larger than the state of Pennsylvania. It is shaped somewhat like the state of California. Its area is 45,483 square miles (117,801 sq km), making it less than one-sixth the size of Zambia, and less than one-third the size of Zimbabwe. It is 520 miles (839 km) long and only from 50 to 100 miles (81 to 162 km) wide. Malawi borders Zambia's east coast. Tanzania is to the north, and Mozambique to the east and south.

Like Zambia, grassland and savanna (areas of coarse grass and trees) cover much of Malawi's land. But there is much scenic beauty, too. Although much of the country is steep and

Zambia borders Lake Tanganyika,
one of the largest lakes in the world,
and one which is known for its
great variety of fish.

rocky, Malawi has some of the most fertile soil in the east-central African region.

The African Rift Valley runs the 500-plus mile (806 km) length of the country from north to south. Lake Malawi, the third largest lake in Africa, stretches to the borders of Tanzania and Mozambique and covers most of the valley. The lake is 350 miles (564 km) long, 10 to 50 miles (16 to 81 km) wide, and 1,550 feet (472 m) above sea level. It has golden beaches, fresh clear water, and is ideal for swimming and fishing. West of the lake, the land rises steeply to a plateau about 4,000 feet (1,220 m) above sea level. To the south is Mount Mlanje, at 9,843 feet (3,002 m) the highest peak in the country.

Although the entire nation lies in the tropics, the climate differs from section to section. In the plateau areas, the temperatures average from about 58° to 65° F (14° to 18° C) annually. The lowlands in the Shire Valley to the south along Lake Malawi have a hot, humid, tropical climate. Here, the temperatures average between 74° and 78° F (23° to 26° C). The northern parts of the country average about 70 inches (179 cm) of rain a year—more than twice as much as in the southwestern section.

While most of Malawi is agricultural and rural in nature, there are some interesting cities, located mostly in scenic pockets of the land. The capital was moved from Zomba in the southern part of the nation to Lilongwe in the central area in 1975. It has a population of more than 100,000. The largest city, and the chief commercial and industrial center of Malawi, is Blantyre, deep in the southern region. Its population is about 230,000. The University of Malawi is located in Zomba, a city of about 25,000 people.

PEOPLE AND CULTURE

Today, there are about seven million people in Zimbabwe. More than six million are native Africans. These are the Mashona peoples—the Karanga, Aezura, Ndau, Manyika, Korekore, and the Ndebele. Smaller ethnic groups include the Tonga, Sena, Hlengwe, Venda, and Sotho.

There are more than half a million white settlers. Most of them arrived during the twentieth century, and great numbers of them fled the country over the past few years during the bloody guerrilla warfare waged by the Africans against the white government. Most of the white population are Europeans, mainly British, Portuguese, Greek, and South African. English is Zimbabwe's main language.

The culture of the Zimbabwe people has been greatly influenced by the Europeans, and the country has a more advanced educational system and a greater degree of industry and technology than most African nations. Examples of traditional native crafts, including wood and soapstone carvings and pottery, can still be found in many areas, however.

Zambia today has a population of over five million. Non-Africans number only about 60,000, mostly Europeans in the mining industry and Asians in business. The main peoples are the Bemba, Tonga, Lozi, Lunda, Luvale, and Nyanja. All these languages are spoken, although English is the country's official language.

While today's African citizens are from many ancestral tribes, the country has a motto which is "One Zambia, one nation." The aim of President Kenneth Kaunda is to build a nonracial society that will not be divided by race, color, or tribal background.

Native Zambian crafts include pottery, spears, basketwork, and masks which are colorfully painted and worn by dancers. Zambians still celebrate each new year by recreating many ancient tribal ceremonies, including a number of interesting dances.

Malawi has a population of more than 5.5 million people, making it one of the most densely populated countries in all Africa. It has more people than Zambia, for example, but only about one-sixth as much land.

Most citizens live in the southern region. The Chewa represent Malawi's largest single ethnic group. They mostly live along the shores of Lake Malawi, and speak ChiChewa, the national language. The Ngoni live in the central region. They are descendents of the legendary Zulu warriors. The Tonga live mainly in the northern region. Other natives include the Tumbuka-Henga and the Ngonde.

Malawi crafts include woven baskets and mats, wood carvings, and beadwork. As in Zambia, dance plays an important part of the social and cultural life of the people. Special dances are held for weddings, funerals, and on many other occasions. Natives wear heavily carved masks and cover themselves with paints and feathers when performing at many ceremonies.

WILDLIFE

Another similarity shared by Zimbabwe, Zambia, and Malawi is the abundance and variety of wildlife that still roams these lands. For example, in Zimbabwe's Wankie National Park alone, near Victoria Falls, there are more than fifty different species of animals. They include lion, eland, giraffe, rhino, zebra, sable, kudu, and waterbuck.

*The Mlanje Mountains in southern
Malawi rise to a height of
almost 10,000 feet (3,000 m).*

At the beautiful Kyle Recreational Park, near Fort Victora in the southeast-central section of Zimbabwe, antelope, giraffe, buffalo, and hippos can be seen. Here also are the rare white rhino, oribi, and nyala. Wildlife is still plentiful in the open countryside and near large cities. In fact, white rhino, zebra, eland, sable, wildbeeste, kudu, and other species are seen near Salisbury and Bulawayo.

A great variety of animals, birds, and fish are found in Zambia. At the Kafue National Park, in the country's western wing, there are buffalo, zebra, warthog, hippopotamus, hartebeest, lion, and many types of antelope. More than 400 species of birds can be seen here, and there are many crocodiles in the rivers.

At the South Luangwa National Park to the east, elephant, lion, giraffe, zebra, black rhino, Cape buffalo, and several types of antelope are found. Most of these species also reside in the Sumbu National Park in the northeast, touching Lake Tanganyika. Here, the fishing is excellent, with bream, Nile perch, lake salmon, and tiger fish.

Malawi has three major game parks, teeming with wildlife. But in this country it is common to sight herds of elephant, eland, and zebra roaming freely across the countryside. At Kasungu National Park in the central region, there are elephant, buffalo, kudu, sable, lion, oribi, zebra, and many smaller species of antelope.

In Malawi more than 900 species of birds have been sighted, and in Lake Malawi there are over 220 species of fish, many of which are not found in any other part of the world.

WEALTH IN THE LAND

There are both similarities and vast differences among Zimbabwe, Zambia, and Malawi regarding natural resources. Zimbabwe and Zambia both have been blessed with rich mineral reserves. Malawi does not have any such reserves, and generally is a much poorer nation than its two neighbors.

ZIMBABWE

Of the three countries, Zimbabwe probably has the best balance of industry and farming. It also has a good supply of natural resources. However, the long fight for independence and control of the country has hurt the economy. Once a lasting peace and freedom come, the nation will regain financial strength.

Zimbabwe has a rich mineral potential. There are some fifty different minerals in the land. For example, the country has 86 percent of the world's known reserves of high-quality chromium. There also are stores of copper, nickel, asbestos, gold, iron, and coal.

A large smelter at Que Que, in the middle of the country, extracts iron from ore mined in the area. Coal comes from the Wankie district in the western region. Over 90 percent of the mined products are exported. But because of the internal strife in Zimbabwe, the mines have not been operated at full capacity in recent years.

Gold was first discovered by Europeans in Zimbabwe in the nineteenth century, and for many years it was a primary source of the nation's wealth. The economic development was spurred greatly around the turn of the century by the rapid construction of railroads. One main line ran up from South Africa, and another in from Mozambique. These provided routes for the exportation of Zimbabwe's natural resources. Coal mining also became important, as coal was used to fuel the railroad locomotives. In contrast, the lack of a good rail system in Zambia slowed that country's economic growth for many years.

In agriculture, too, there is a rich abundance. Zimbabwe raises enough crops to feed its own population and also export some products. One of the most important exports has been tobacco, which grows well under the ideal climate conditions. Other major agricultural crops are sugar, corn, cotton, peanuts, tea, and wheat.

Tourism also was once a major industry in Zimbabwe. But with all the recent fighting and unrest, this has fallen off sharply over the past several years.

Even with the troubles of the past two decades, Zimbabwe still is more developed and industrialized than its neighbors to the north. The Kariba Gorge hydroelectric plant on the Zambezi River is one of the world's largest. The dam here forms Kariba Lake, which covers 2,000 square miles (5,180 sq km). The plant supplies electricity to most of the country.

ZAMBIA

Much of Zambia's economy can be summed up in one word—copper. This valuable resource has been mined in the country for over two thousand years and today remains the number one product by far. Copper represents as much as 90 percent of Zambia's annual exports. The copper is of high quality, with a natural high resistance to corrosion. This gives it a longer life and makes it especially suitable for conducting heat and electricity.

Four large copper mines and several smaller ones are concentrated in the Copperbelt province near the Zaire border to the north. Here, in an area approximately 30 by 90 miles (48 by 145 km), both open pit and underground mining are done.

Such heavy dependence on one resource, however great the supply and quality are, can cause problems with the national economy. Shortly after World War II there was a big copper boom. Greater supplies of the metal were needed to feed the fast-growing automobile and electrical industries. Zambia's mines were then very profitable. But when the world price of copper is down, Zambia suffers. Therefore, the government has been trying to develop other industrial and agricultural means of support.

There are other reserves in the country. South of the Copperbelt, Zambia has lead and zinc mines. Large coal deposits are located near Kariba Lake.

Fishing is an important industry: in the Luapula province from Lake Bangweulu; in the Northern province from Lake Tanganyika; and in the Western province from the Zambezi River.

Only certain areas of Zambia are good for farming. Enough wheat is raised to feed the population, but many other foods have to be imported. Much of the agricultural production, including cotton, is in the Central province. Other products include tobacco, corn, and cashew nuts.

Overall, however, much of the Zambian soil is poor for farming. Recently, the government has made a determined effort to train experts in agriculture, but this has not been too successful. There is still a shortage of such experts, of modern farming equipment, and of good roads to transport products to the cities.

Zambia today continues to rely too strongly on its copper production. To move forward, the country must find ways to develop a more rounded economic base.

MALAWI

Malawi is a poor country. It does not have any rich mineral resources stored in its land. The nation has always depended upon agriculture as its most important activity. Even today, more than 90 percent of the population is directly dependent upon agriculture, although only about one-third of Malawi is suitable for farming. However, the government is developing programs to use more land and to get maximum crop yield from the land already being used.

The fact that Malawi does have a good variety of crops is a help. Thus if one crop is hurt by poor harvests or low market prices, other crops will still keep the economy stable. Maize (corn) is the main food crop and is grown on almost all small farms. It accounts for 75 percent of all land under cultivation.

Other food crops include rice, groundnuts (peanuts), cassava, millet, sorghum, sweet potatoes, coffee, and some fruit. Tobacco, tea, sugar, groundnuts, cotton, rice, and sunflower seeds are exported. In addition, there are nearly one million head of cattle, and a great number of pigs, sheep, goats, and poultry in Malawi.

Commercial fishing, especially from Lake Malawi, is becoming an important industry, and adds to the variety of the diet for the people. There is also some small industry in the country. This mainly includes foodstuffs, cotton textiles, cigarettes, maize meal, sugar, canned fish and fruit, bricks, timber, metal products, and matches. The government also has programs underway aimed at promoting tourism. With Lake Malawi, three national parks, and a scenic countryside, there is much to offer tourists.

4
BANTU BEGINNINGS

Little is known about the ancient past of south-central Africa, including the lands of Zimbabwe, Zambia, and Malawi. There are some key clues that link back several hundred, even thousands, of years ago, but even these are often confusing and mysterious.

In Zimbabwe, for example, more than two thousand rock paintings have been found in caves throughout the country. Some experts believe these to be the work of primitive bushmen who may have painted them as early as five thousand to six thousand years before the birth of Christ. Ancient tools also have been found.

According to many historians some of the earliest settlers in this area of Africa belonged to the Bantu speaking people. Nearly one-third of all Africans speak one form or another of the Bantu language. It is believed the Bantu lived in the Ni-

These paintings, found on the walls of a cave in Zimbabwe, are believed to have been made by bushmen about 4,000 years ago.

geria-Cameroon area of Africa, the upper-middle western section, somewhere between 1000 and 500 B.C. Around 500 B.C., their expanding population forced the Bantu to seek new lands for farming and hunting.

The Atlantic Ocean blocked movement to the southwest, and other people already occupied the vast plains to the north and east. The only possible route was south. Over the next several centuries the Bantus slowly moved down into the heart of Central Africa. There is some evidence that they may have reached the territory that is now Zimbabwe, Zambia, and Malawi about two thousand years ago.

Sometime during the first or second century an early people in Zambia began to mine and use iron. They lived in villages built on mounds, and began to develop a culture that has some similarities to the present-day Tonga natives who live in Zambia's Southern province.

It is generally agreed that by 500 A.D., the Bantus had settled over a large belt of Central Africa, stretching between the Atlantic and Indian Oceans. This included large parts of Zimbabwe, Zambia, and Malawi. Areas rich in soil and ample in rainfall became the heaviest populated and prospered. The Bantu mixed with natives they found in the area, teaching them their skills in farming, pottery, and ironworking.

Zimbabwe and Zambia each proved to be a rich source of minerals in the earth. There is evidence that extensive mining activity took place in these countries for more than a thousand years. Arab traders dealt in the buying and selling of these minerals on the coast near Zimbabwe as early as 700 A.D.

One of the great mysteries of this region of Africa lies at a site near Fort Victoria in southeastern Zimbabwe. Here, rising eerily from the plains are the massive stone ruins of what, centuries ago, was a magnificent, fortress-like complex. In fact, Zimbabwe is a word translated by some as "houses of stone," and by others as "great house." The country took its name from these stone monuments of another era.

It is not known exactly when these works originally were built, although some experts believe the first stone walls may have been put up as early as 300 to 400 A.D. The ruins stretch over more than 60 acres (24 hectares). The giant stone walls are 30 feet high (9.15 m) and 14 feet (4.2 m) thick in some places. A 32-foot-high (9.76 m) tower still stands. There are ruins of what once may have been a great temple, 292 feet (89 m) long and 220 feet (67 m) wide.

The oldest parts of the ruins are on a hill and are called "The Acropolis." This is thought to have been an important religious center, and possibly the burial place of great chiefs.

Surrounding this area there are about three hundred smaller ruins crowning hills and nestling in valleys, all made of stone and all of the same general design. Early explorers found gold ornaments and other valuable objects of art in many of the sites.

It is obvious that whoever did build the walls and the buildings was highly skilled in the art of stoneworking. No mortar or even mud was used to hold the stones together. Stone buildings were almost unheard-of south of the Sahara Desert. And there are no other ruins of such scale anywhere in Africa south of the Pyramids of Egypt. An advanced civilization must have built the stone walls, towers, and temples. But who? And why? The riddle remains unsolved today.

The Bantu peoples and their descendents apparently lived

in relative peace for centuries. The entire Zimbabwe region, including Zambia and parts of Malawi, was a major center of Bantu civilization between 400 A.D. and 1900 A.D., with the peak development occurring between 1400 and 1800.

In the 1500s and 1600s, first explorers, then settlers from several European countries began to recognize the rich potential of land and resources that lay almost untapped in Africa. They began moving into the coastal areas and taking over the territory, killing or enslaving the native population. They claimed the new land in the name of their mother countries—Portugal, Holland, Spain, France, and England, among others.

But for another three hundred or so years, the tribes in the area that is now Zimbabwe, Zambia, and Malawi continued to live mostly in peace. The Europeans did not bother them until much later because these lands were difficult to reach. They were far from the coasts. Early explorers were attacked by wild animals and hostile natives, and were stricken with tropical diseases. For example, the Dutch began settlement of South Africa in the middle of the seventeenth century, but it would be more than another two hundred years before colonists would push far enough north to reach Zimbabwe.

Actually, the Portuguese were the first Europeans to try to tame this wild country. They had settled in Angola to the west and in Mozambique to the east. Early in the eighteenth century they tried to move into Zambia and open up a route from the Atlantic Ocean to the Indian Ocean, principally for slave trading, which was a big business at the time. But conditions in this interior land were so difficult and dangerous that they soon abandoned the idea and left.

5

FREEDOM LOST, AND WON

Two white men, born in the British Isles forty years apart in the nineteenth century, had enormous influence on the modern history of south-central Africa. This impact is still felt today.

One was David Livingstone, a Scotsman, born in 1813. The other was Cecil Rhodes, born in England in 1853. These two men were worlds apart in their ideals and goals. But both were iron-willed, courageous each in his own way, and they were both strong, adventurous leaders.

David Livingstone was among other things, a medical missionary, explorer, geographer, botanist, geologist, historian, and humanitarian. He first went to Africa in 1841, to teach Christianity, civilization, and commerce to the tribal peoples and to try and stop slave trading.

In 1851, Livingstone first sighted the Zambezi River in what is now Zambia. He was so impressed with the great river that he said: "How glorious! How magnificent! How beautiful." For the next two decades, until his death in 1873, he spent almost all the rest of his life exploring and living in Zambia, Malawi, and some parts of northern Zimbabwe.

It was a rugged life. He traveled thousands of miles through swamps, desert, mountains, and prairies on foot. He encountered wild animals, hostile native tribes, and disease, yet he continued his march. He taught Christianity and practiced modern medicine where for hundreds of years witch doctors had ruled. Against great odds, he fought merciless slave traders. He brought education and learning to people who had never known how to read or write.

Livingstone crossed the continent from coast to coast, clearing up the mystery of the interior lands to Europeans. He encouraged settlers to come in and help with the missionary work. In 1855, he discovered Victoria Falls, and in 1859 he discovered Lake Malawi.

Sometimes, his friends and relatives in Scotland and England would not hear from him for months or years at a time. Once, a newspaper sent Henry Stanley to Africa to find Livingstone after a long period of no word from the explorer. Several months later Stanley found him in a small native village and said the famous words, "Dr. Livingstone, I presume."

The spectacular Victoria Falls, discovered in 1855 by David Livingstone, is one of the great tourist attractions of Zambia.

Livingstone died in the Africa he loved in 1873. Although there would be more than a century of unrest and uprisings between whites and natives, Livingstone still is remembered for the love and friendship he inspired. A town in southern Zambia, near Victoria Falls, is named Livingstone in his honor.

CECIL RHODES

Cecil Rhodes influenced the future of this region of Africa in a different way. He first went to South Africa in 1870, and began working in the diamond mines at Kimberly. Soon, he had made a fortune and controlled almost all of the diamonds produced in the world.

In the 1880s he went north to Zimbabwe and forced the Matabele tribe to surrender most of its land to Great Britain. Soon after, Lewanika, the powerful chief of the Barotse people in what is now the Western province of Zambia, was tricked into signing land and mining and farming rights over to Rhodes' assistants. This led to the creation of the state of Rhodesia, named after Rhodes and including at the time Zimbabwe and Zambia. Zimbabwe, a century ago, was known as Matabeleland, named after the Matabele natives who lived there. Zambia was then known as Barotseland, named after the Barotse tribe.

Rhodes was one of the first to realize the full potential of the rich mineral assets that lay in these lands. He helped form the British South Africa Company, which more or less ruled the lands and people of Zimbabwe and Zambia from 1890 to the 1920s.

Rhodes not only laid plans for large-scale mining, but also set up the transportation systems needed to get such metals as gold, copper, and chromium across country to the coast for shipments to Great Britain and to other parts of the world.

But Rhodes had even higher ambitions. He wanted to build a great railroad from Cairo, Egypt, in the north, to the southern tip of Africa. In this he failed, but his efforts left lasting scars on the region. Rhodes was a tyrant who bullied natives and other European settlers alike to get his way. He believed that white men should rule Africans even though it was the Africans' homeland. His policies, continued long after his death in 1902, helped create racial unrest that still exists today, particularly in Zimbabwe.

At about the same time that Rhodes was pushing forth in Zimbabwe and Zambia, another Englishman, Sir Harry Johnston, began taking over land in Malawi. He made treaties with all the leading chiefs living in a large area stretching from the Shire Highlands along the western shores of Lake Malawi to the southern end of Lake Tanganyika. The country became a British protectorate in 1891.

Rhodes and Johnston were slowly taking over these lands in the name of Great Britain. They convinced the native chiefs in the area that it would be best for their peoples to be under British protection. This, they promised, would save them from invasions by other European powers.

The takeover of Zimbabwe, Zambia, and Malawi during this period, like the takeover of most of the rest of Africa by Europeans, was much like what happened in America when the first white settlers came in and pushed native Americans off their land.

The African chiefs had been promised many good things for their people by Rhodes, Johnston, and others. The Europeans told them they would teach them modern mining and farming methods and would educate their children.

Instead, the British settlers grabbed the best farming lands for themselves, leaving the poorer lands for the Africans. They stole cattle from the natives, forced them into slave-like labor, and placed heavy taxes on them. Permanent white settlements were established, and if the Africans complained, they were beaten, jailed, or killed.

Soon, the British, who represented only a very small percentage of the total population, completely took over rule of the land, stripping long-proud chiefs of their authority. In short, the Africans became second-class citizens in their own homeland.

By the mid-1890s, the conquest of these lands had been completed. In 1896, people from the Shona, Ndebele, and other area tribes, finally revolted in Zimbabwe. They attacked white settlements and slaughtered men, women, and children. The British, with the help of European volunteers from South Africa, turned back the rebellion and drove the natives into retreat. Smaller revolts in Zambia and Malawi were also broken during these years. By the turn of the twentieth century, most of the resistance had been defeated. In 1898, Great Britain recognized Southern Rhodesia (Zimbabwe) and Northern Rhodesia (Zambia) as separate territories.

The total unfairness of foreign rule in these African countries, and the pitiful state of the Africans, was well expressed by events which occurred in Nyasaland (Malawi) early in the twentieth century. John Chilembwe, an African who was educated in the United States, became a leader among his people.

For years he had seen sad examples of how the Africans were brutally used and abused by Europeans. When World War I broke out in Europe it was followed, in the fall of 1914, by fierce fighting between British and German forces in northern

Nyasaland. Chilembwe was deeply upset that Africans, forced into the fighting, were being killed and wounded for a cause in which they had no interest.

"Let the rich men, bankers, titled men, storekeepers, farmers, and landlords go to war and get shot," he wrote. "Instead, the poor Africans who have nothing to win in this present world . . . are invited to die for a cause which is not theirs."

Chilembwe wanted his statement to be published in the local newspaper, but it was refused. He decided the only way to show the unfairness of his people's situation was through armed revolt. He told his followers: "You must not think that you are going to defeat white men and then become kings of your own country. All we can hope for is that the white man will think, after we are dead, that the treatment they are giving our people is bad and they might change."

Soon after, however, Chilembwe was shot while trying to escape to Mozambique, and the small uprising was put down. He became a folk hero in his country, but once again the African people were defeated in their attempt to gain respect and equal rights in their own homeland.

The British South Africa Company ceased to rule the Rhodesians in 1922. The white settlers voted for self-government, and Southern Rhodesia (Zimbabwe) became a self-governing British colony in 1923. Northern Rhodesia (Zambia) became a British colony a year later.

The discovery of large copper ore deposits in Zambia in the late 1920s brought in a rush of even more Europeans, and within ten years, mining was an established industry.

For the most part, things were generally quiet under British rule for the next quarter of a century, extending through World

War II. A few years after the war, however, as the seeds of independence were beginning to sprout in other parts of Africa, the white European settlers asked for more control and protection from Great Britain. As a result, Northern and Southern Rhodesia and Nyasaland were formed, in 1953, into a Federation. The Africans opposed this because a small minority of whites still controlled the government.

For a few years the Federation prospered. There was an economic boom following World War II. By the mid-1950s, Southern Rhodesia had become the most highly industrialized country in tropical Africa, and hundreds of thousands of native children were enrolled in schools. In Northern Rhodesia, copper production doubled in the years between 1946 and 1956, greatly increasing the wealth of that country.

Even with this growth, however, the Federation lasted only ten years. It broke up in 1963, mainly because Southern Rhodesia was getting far more than its share of benefits, including British funds, than either Northern Rhodesia or Nyasaland. By the 1960s, too, many other African nations had engaged in long bloody battles for their independence, and Britain saw that its days of colonization in Africa were numbered. Steps were taken to prepare the Africans to regain control of their native land.

INDEPENDENCE

On July 6, 1964, Malawi was declared an independent nation. Two years later a new constitution was drawn up and Malawi became a republic. Its new president was Dr. Hastings Kamuzu Banda, a medical doctor who had been a leader in his country's long fight for freedom.

Despite the independence, however, Malawi people today

face some difficult problems. Because the nation does not possess the rich natural resources of some of its neighboring countries, more than 90 percent of the population are directly dependent upon agriculture for their living. Large, privately owned tea, tobacco and sugar estates have done quite well in recent years, but the small farmer is having a hard time making ends meet. As one consequence of this, the government has placed a low priority on primary education and preventive medicine, giving a higher budget to improve agricultural production. While this emphasis may help solve more immediate needs, it hurts the long range future of Malawi by insuring a relatively high rate of illiteracy and poor health care, particularly among the young.

Northern Rhodesia became independent and changed its name to Zambia on October 24, 1964. Kenneth Kaunda, an ex-schoolteacher who also had long fought for native rule of his homeland, was named the first president of Zambia. He declared a national policy of humanism. This policy is based on the way of life that was common in Africa before the Europeans took control. That is, all citizens work together with the common goal of providing a good life for every individual. The government has the responsibility of seeing that everyone is cared for in as equal a manner as possible.

However, Zambia has major problems yet to solve that have kept many of its people mired in poverty. The country's dependence on copper has created an economic imbalance. Because the copperbelt areas have thrived, tens of thousands of natives streamed out of rural areas to swell mining towns and cities. Not only did this create a shortage of workers in the less populated agricultural regions, but the massive migration led to

*During Zimbabwe's recent civil strife, young people
moved to refugee camps in nearby Zambia.
Children of a war-torn era, these refugee boys
carved imitation guns out of wood.*

ghettolike conditions in the cities. As a result, education, health care, and agriculture have all suffered, and will likely continue to until a better spread of the national economy can be achieved.

Events took a far different turn in Southern Rhodesia in the mid-1960s. The white minority still ruled the government, and demanded that Britain declare the nation independent. The British, though, were not happy with the unrepresentative government, and wanted Africans to have a greater voice in the running of the country.

No agreement could be reached, and on November 11, 1965, Rhodesian prime minister Ian Smith declared Rhodesia independent. Great Britain termed this action illegal. Within a few months, Britain banned all trade with Rhodesia, including precious oil supplies. The United Nations Security Council also urged all countries to stop trading with Rhodesia.

Stubbornly, Smith and the minority government held control of the country, although the trade restrictions caused the economy to suffer greatly. Worse, the long simmering unrest among the black African majority in Rhodesia now reached boiling point. Rebel groups sprung up throughout the land, launching attacks on white settlements.

Zambia's economy also suffered, because its government supported the Africans in Rhodesia. So the white-controlled government in Rhodesia closed its borders to Zambia and would no longer allow the transportation of copper from Zambia through Rhodesia to the coast for export all over the world.

This uneasy situation lasted through the 1970s, and caused a great amount of bloodshed, especially from 1973 through 1979, when an open state of guerrilla warfare existed. In 1979, the first signs of a peace settlement occurred. Bishop Abel

*Prime Minister Robert Mugabe of Zimbabwe
chats with President Jimmy Carter during
an August 1980 visit to Washington.*

Muzorewa was named the first black prime minister in the country's history.

Then, in December 1979, with the help of the British, who acted as peacemakers, a truce was declared. Rebel leaders Robert Mugabe and Joshua Nkomo agreed to a cease-fire leading to the holding of free and fair elections in 1980 whereby the Africans would gain majority control of the government. The country would no longer be known as Rhodesia. It would be known as Zimbabwe; named for a civilization that had lived there centuries ago.

As the 1980s began, there was hope of a lasting peace in this long-troubled land. Early in 1980, Mugabe was elected Prime Minister. He immediately called for peace. "There is room for everyone in a new society," he said. "Today, white or black, we are all Zimbabweans."

Despite its rich natural resources, the country today still faces a long, uphill struggle to regain its strength. Throughout the land, especially in rural areas, malnutrition and disease are common. Half of the black population lives on land that is agriculturally exhausted. The birthrate is among the highest in the world, with half the population currently under age fifteen. The illiteracy rate is high; education and health care are poor and will take years to rebuild. In Zimbabwe, the cost of precious freedom was high. With well-managed government, however, the country has the resources to become prosperous in time.

6

THE GIANT ISLAND

Lying 250 miles (403 km) off the southeast coast of Africa is the giant island of Madagascar. Today, it is also known as the Malagasy Republic. It has an area of 228,000 square miles (590,520 sq km), slightly smaller than the state of Texas. In fact, Madagascar is the fourth largest island in the world. Only Greenland, New Guinea, and Borneo are bigger.

The island is shaped almost like a huge left footprint, with the big toe pointing north. It is about 1,000 miles (1,613 km) long and 360 miles (581 km) across at the widest point. It is separated from the African mainland by the Mozambique Channel.

More than nine million people live here. The main languages are Malagasy (a mixture of Malay and Indonesian), and French. Half of the islanders are Christians. The rest practice ancient tribal religions.

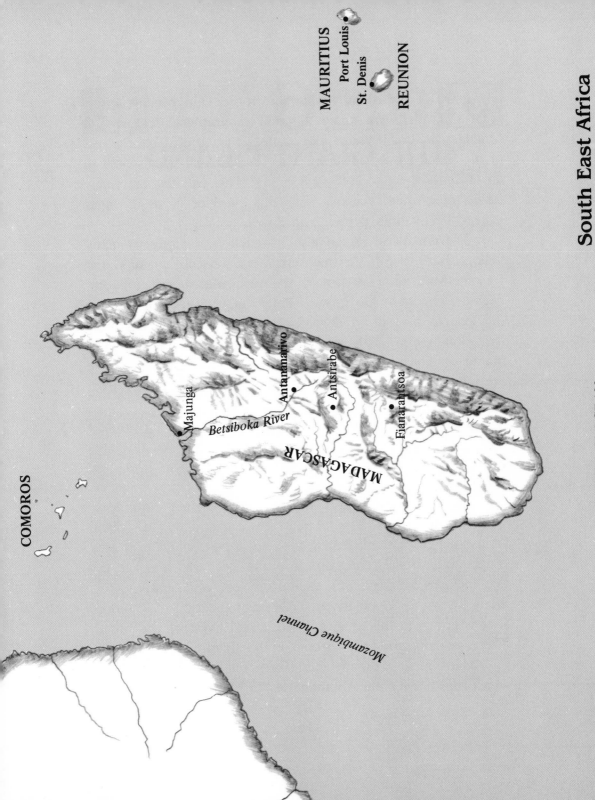

MAURITIUS

Port Louis

St. Denis

REUNION

COMOROS

Majunga

Betsiboka River

Antananarivo

Antsirabe

MADAGASCAR

Fianarantsoa

Mozambique Channel

INDIAN OCEAN

South East Africa

Madagascar

Most of the island lies in the tropics, but because of its great size, there are many different geographical features on Madagascar. For instance, the north end is cut off from the rest of the island by the towering Mt. Tsaratanana, which rises to an altitude of 9,450 feet (2,882 m). This end has extremely fertile valleys and volcanic soils that produce crops of sugar cane, coffee, vanilla, pepper, and cloves.

The northwest region also has rich land along its many valleys. Here, rice is the main crop, but tobacco, peanuts, and some cotton also are grown. In the western area, rice, tobacco, peanuts, and corn are grown. Three large rivers run through the western part of Madagascar and in recent years a large irrigation system has been developed, which will produce even more rice. The west coast is hotter than the east coast and there are long rainy and dry seasons. Temperatures may vary from 50° to 100° F (10° to 38° C).

The south is an arid region. Here, more irrigation projects have made the raising of rice and corn possible. But this area is better known for large deposits of coal, mica, iron, and manganese.

The east coast region has many fertile areas and dense tropical rain forests. The climate is warm and humid. Inland from either coast, roads lead to the central plateau, a cooler area ranging in altitude from 2,000 to 4,000 feet (610 to 1,220 m) that includes Madagascar's capital city of Antananarivo (formerly known as Tananarive). It has a population of 400,000. Rice is grown in this area, and cattle and livestock are raised. There are more cattle than people on the island.

Madagascar has many great rivers. The longest is the Ikopa, which runs north from Antananarivo to Majunga, a distance of more than 150 miles (242 km). Some of these rivers have beautiful falls, such as Namorona and Sakaleona. There also are a number of lakes.

Overall, the island has beautiful coasts, interesting wildlife, and mountain scenery. This has led to a rise in tourism in recent years. However, most natives of Madagascar still live in rural conditions, with farming and herding as the chief occupations. The most important crop is rice, followed by coffee, vanilla, cotton, beans, and sugar. Madagascar is the world's largest producer of vanilla.

There is also a good variety of minerals on the island, but the sites are scattered and the resources are not in large enough deposits to mine economically. Some graphite, mica, and bauxite are exported.

The wildlife includes the interesting monkey-like lemur with a foxlike head, the weasel-like fosa, crocodile, bushpig, and guinea fowl. About 300 different species of birds can be sighted on Madagascar. More than 1,000 years ago the largest bird in the world roamed through the island's rain forests. It was called *Aepyornis maximus,* stood more than 9 feet tall (nearly 3 m), and weighed 1,000 pounds (almost half a metric ton.)

HISTORY

Madagascar has a colorful and somewhat mysterious history. No trace of prehistoric man has been found on the island, and just who the first inhabitants were is not known even today. It has been established, however, that thousands of tan-skinned natives of Malaya, Indonesia, and Polynesia in southern Asia migrated to Madagascar between 200 B.C. and 800 A.D. They came across the ocean in huge outrigger canoes, each capable of

holding up to two hundred people. They brought with them their language, customs, and a style of farming. Most of them settled in the central highlands near Antananarivo. Large square family tombs of these ancient families can still be seen around the capital city.

Arabs and Africans settled along the coasts of the island as early as the ninth century, but Europeans did not discover Madagascar until the year 1500. Over the next 300 years the Portuguese, the French, and the British tried to establish settlements, but all failed.

Then for a number of years, from the latter part of the seventeenth century into the early part of the eighteenth century, Madagascar became the launching base for bands of sea pirates, including the famous Captain William Kidd. They attacked the merchant ships laden with rich goods headed for Europe. Only when the great European powers sent increasing numbers of warships to the area did the pirate activity die out.

Meanwhile, the natives of the island, called Malagasians, developed several rival kingdoms. These were largely unified in the year 1787 into the Merina kingdom by a great leader. His name was Andrianampoinimerina. He and his son, Radama I, ruled until 1828, and in the process brought together many of the warring tribes under one leadership. Radama's wife, Ranavalona, ruled as Queen from 1828 until 1861. During this

A woman in Madagascar strips and cleans old sisal ropes so that they can be rewound and used again.

restless period she led a campaign against European mission-
aries and settlers, and drove most of them from the island.

After she died in 1861, however, the Europeans returned,
and the French in particular gained influence. This led to the
Franco-Malagasy wars in the 1880s and 1890s. The French
won and made Madagascar one of their colonies in 1896.

For the next fifty years the French continued their rule over
the Malagasy people, causing much bitterness and resentment
on the part of the islanders. Such deep feelings led, finally, to a
major revolt in 1947. The French sent in troops to regain control, and tens of thousands of islanders were killed or starved
to death during the fighting. But it was now obvious, even to the
French, that a final peace on Madagascar would not be achieved
until independence was granted.

Slowly, the steps to this freedom were taken. In 1956, a local
government council was set up and given some power to ad-
minister laws. Two years later, Madagascar became the Malagasy Republic, a self-governing body in the French community.
Full independence was granted on June 26, 1960. Today, the
Malagasy Republic includes Madagascar and small nearby
islands.

The new freedom has not been easy for the Malagasians.
Political fighting broke out in 1972 and again in 1975. This produced a new democratic republic and a new constitution. Today,
85 percent of the island's population live in poor, rural conditions, and many young people are forced to work in the
fields before they can get a good education. The illiteracy rate
remains high by world standards and will probably stay high
until the Malagasy economy can be broadened, creating new
growth opportunities for the nine million proud people of this
giant island off the east coast of Africa.

PEOPLE AND CULTURE

These people, although geographically isolated from the rest of the world for centuries, were civilized long before the French took over in 1896. And they retain many of their ancestral cultures and traditions today.

Unlike many people on the mainland of Africa, for instance, the Malagasy people were able to read and write long before the Europeans settled there. The Merina king Radama I had the wisdom to educate his people in the early 1800s.

The Malagasy also excel in many forms of art. This, too, was introduced during the reign of Radama I. Many of the early paintings reflect the history and life style of the island people. There are many sculptors also, skilled in stone and wood carvings. This art form apparently dates back several hundred years, as small stone fertility charms and human and animal figures have been found dating to ancient times.

Music is another important custom in the Malagasy folklore. Wandering minstrels still play through the countryside. Each district has musicians who play at important festivals, including marriages, births, and funerals.

As on the continent of Africa, dancing is a key form of cultural expression on Madagascar. There is a great variety of dance forms on the island reflecting the various ethnic backgrounds of the people—Indonesian, Arab, and African. The Merina dances, for example, are accompanied by musical instruments that link back to Asian traditions. But the Bara, Antandroy, and Mahafaly dances on the southern end of the island are more spirited, following the beat of drums in the African manner.

Malagasy craftsmen create fine, delicate bracelets, necklaces, and earrings from native gold filled with precious stones. Island women wear long beaded necklaces and bracelets

A typical herder's brush shelter in southern Madagascar.

made from wood, shells, and beads. Wood craftsmen create a variety of statuettes, lamp bases, wooden beds, and small chests.

Interesting souvenirs of the island include turtle shells, large butterflies mounted in frames, model boats, and beautiful seashells. Woven baskets and straw hats are also found at markets throughout the countryside.

The most common item of Malagasy clothing is the lamba. This is a cloth shawl worn over the shoulder by men and women. Women carry babies in lambas, and the dead are wrapped in lambas before they are placed inside tombs. Usually white, some lambas are woven of attractive silk and often are worn on Sundays.

7
SUGARCANE CAPITAL

The smaller islands of Mauritius and Réunion—the Mascarenes —lie farther east, like a pair of acorn-shaped cuff links, rising out of the Indian Ocean. Mauritius is the slightly larger of the two. It is about 720 square miles (1,865 sq km), or roughly half the size of Rhode Island.

It is further out than Réunion, about 500 miles east (806 km) of Madagascar; 1,000 miles (1,613 km) from the African mainland; and nearly 2,500 miles (4,032 km) southwest of India. It stands on what was once a land bridge between Africa and Asia. This is known as the Mascarene archipelago.

Mauritius has been called "a pearl in the Indian Ocean," and an "island of rainbows." This is because even though it is of volcanic origin, and is surrounded by coral reefs, it is a scenic island with beautiful white and golden beaches, blue seas, and deep lagoons. It also is favored with a mild climate, constantly cooled by soft ocean breezes. The coasts are warm year-round, with temperatures averaging from the mid-70s to the low 80s, Fahrenheit (23 to 29° C). These attractions, in recent years, have triggered an important new industry for the island— tourism.

However, the main business on Mauritius is, and always has been, sugarcane. In fact, the island's economy rises and falls with the fortunes of the world sugar market. When this market is good, nearly everyone prospers on the island. But when the market is bad, nearly everyone suffers.

From the coast, the land rises to form a broad, fertile plateau, 2,000 feet (610 m) and more above sea level, filled with endless rows of sugarcane. Sugar covers 90 percent of the farming land, and makes up nearly 90 percent of Mauritius' exports.

In the past few years the government has encouraged more variety in industry and agriculture to build a better economic base for the island. Tourism helps. Tea is becoming an important export, and some small industries have started up. Still Mauritius is heavily dependent upon imports from other lands to feed its rapidly-growing population. The capital of Mauritius is Port Louis, a busy port city of nearly 150,000 people about one-third of the way down the island's west coast.

In comparison to Zimbabwe, Zambia, Malawi, and Madagascar, there is relatively little wildlife on Mauritius. It once was the home of the now extinct dodo bird and the giant land tortoise. Today, only deer, monkeys, and rabbits are found on the island. Offshore fishing is excellent, however, and provides food for the population. The seas teem with tuna, barracuda, bonito, kingfish, and blue marlin.

The independent nation of Mauritius also includes some

smaller islands. The most important of these is Rodriques, about 300 miles (484 km) to the east. It has about 250,000 farmers and villagers. Cargados Carajos Shoals and Agalega lie far to the northeast and north. These lonely dots in the Indian Ocean are the home for small crews of fishermen and plantation workers.

HISTORY

Portuguese sailors first stepped foot on the island of Mauritius sometime in the sixteenth century. They stopped for food and water on the long sea journey from the Cape of Good Hope at the tip of South Africa to the East Indies. Still, no one lived on the island until the Dutch claimed it in 1598, naming it Mauritius after Prince Maurice of Nassau.

The Dutch brought in slaves from Madagascar to cut down ebony forests and sent the valuable wood back to Europe. They left Mauritius in 1710 and the French moved in and took over in 1715. French colonists from the neighboring island of Bourbon (Réunion) settled here. They brought in more slaves, built a port, and planted coffee, fruit, spices, sugar, and vegetables.

Because of the important location of the island, it was used by the French as a launching base for attacks against British ships and against British settlements across the ocean in India.

A Mauritian couple carry fresh sugarcane past the remains of ancient volcanoes. The soft outer cones of the volcanoes have eroded away, leaving hardened lava cores.

This occurred during the Anglo-French wars of the 1700s. The British finally captured the island in 1810 and made it a colony.

By this time sugarcane had become a big business. A few years later the British freed all the slaves on Mauritius. Sugar plantation owners then had to find new workers for the fields. From 1835 to 1907, these planters brought in nearly half a million laborers from India. Many of these people raised families and remained on the island after their work contracts ran out.

Thus the population of Mauritius today is a cultural mix of Indian, French, British, Malagasian, Chinese, and African. The majority of Mauritians today are Hindu, descendants of laborers transported from India in the nineteenth century. The most widely spoken language is Creole, a blend of French, Bantu, and Malagasy. English and French are also taught in schools and are widely used.

After World War II, Great Britain began a process to allow Mauritians to govern themselves. This led to the island's independence in 1968.

Today, there is a popular slogan that well describes the island. It is "The East meets the West in Mauritius." Although its peoples have cultures and religions that vary greatly, all live together peacefully. This sets an example that would be well for the rest of the world to observe and follow.

The milkman travels by bicycle on the island of Mauritius, delivering milk from a container fastened to the front of the seat.

However, with nearly one million people, Mauritius has a serious problem of overpopulation. This is causing much unemployment, widespread poverty, and poor living conditions, which lead to disease and poor health in some areas. These conditions and the lack of educational opportunities have led to some political unrest. Until a way is found to broaden the island's economy, now so heavily dependent on sugarcane, this situation is likely to continue.

8
RESTFUL RÉUNION

The island of Réunion, which lies less than 500 miles (806 km) from the eastern coast of Madagascar, is slightly smaller than Mauritius. It covers 969 square miles (2,510 sq km). It also is an island of volcanic origin.

There are two mountain masses on Réunion. One is in the northeast, and the highest peak rises more than 10,000 feet (3,048 m). In the southeast is a still-active volcano 8,160 feet (2,489 m) high. Between these two masses is a high plain, almost a mile above sea level.

Like its neighbor, Mauritius, Réunion has a tropical climate with a year-round temperature average of 69°F (21° C). Thick forests blanket the interior of the island. Most of the people live along the coasts, which feature fine sand beaches, separated from the ocean by coral reefs.

Also like Mauritius, Réunion depends heavily upon its sugarcane crop. This covers more than two-thirds of the island's cultivated land, and accounts for nearly 90 percent of all exports. Thus, Réunion too has an economy dependent upon the sugar market. When the world price is down, Réunion suffers.

In addition to sugarcane, tropical fruits, vegetables, vanilla, and perfumes are also exported. Cattle, pigs, goats, and sheep are raised, especially in the lush high plains area. In recent years, two promising new industries have begun. One is deep-sea fishing. Fishing ports have been built at Saint-leu and at Saint-Gilles. The other new industry is tourism. Europeans in particular have found Réunion's beaches a relaxing place to visit.

HISTORY

No one lived on Réunion when the Portuguese navigator Pedro de Mascarenhas, for whom the Mascarene Islands were named, discovered it in 1528. The French first settled there in the middle of the seventeenth century and named the island Ile Bourbon. Later, rich sugarcane plantations were established. To work them, Africans, Madagascans, Chinese, and Indians migrated to the island. Over the centuries these races have mixed to form a varied population.

The island has been ruled by the French government throughout its history, except for a brief period from 1810 to 1815, when it was occupied by the British. Today it is governed as an Overseas Department of France, although there is a movement among the island's people to become independent.

Réunion has a population of about half a million people. Nearly 100,000 live in the capital of Saint-Denis, on the tip of the northern coast. A large percentage of the population, about half, is made up of young people under 21 years old. Unemployment is a chronic problem, a fact that puts a strain on the island's economy as well as on its social structure. The use of modern technology and equipment on large cane plantations has caused great numbers of day laborers to lose their jobs. This problem is compounded by Réunion's high population growth rate, which has been triggered in part by lack of good formal education programs. Such depressing conditions have forced many young people on the island to emigrate to France. Officials are developing plans to expand the island's economic base, hopefully developing work for more people.

FOR FURTHER READING

BOOKS

Dresang, Eliza T. *The Land and People of Zambia.* New York: J. B. Lippincott, 1975.

Magary, Alan and Kerstin Magary. *East Africa: A Travel Guide.* New York: Harper and Row, 1975.

Murphy, E. Jefferson. *The Bantu Civilization of Southern Africa* New York: Thomas Y. Crowell, 1974.

Sterling, Thomas. *Exploration of Africa.* New York: American Heritage, 1963.

Traveller's Guide to Africa 1980. London: IC Magazines Ltd., Yearly

Valkos, Olivia. *African Beginnings.* New York: Penguin Press, 1977.

PERIODICALS AND PAMPHLETS

"Give Rhodesia a Chance." *Reader's Digest,* August, 1978.

Facts about the Democratic Republic of Madagascar. (Embassy of the Democratic Republic of Madagascar, 2374 Massachusetts Ave., NW, Washington, D.C. 20008)

A History of the Democratic Republic of Madagascar.

The Island of Réunion. (French Government Tourist Office, 610 Fifth Avenue, New York, N.Y. 10020)

"Madagascar: Island at the End of the Earth." *National Geographic,* October, 1967.

Malawi: The Year in Review. (The Embassy of Malawi, 1400 20th St., NW, Washington, D.C. 20036)

Mauritius Pocket Guide. (The Embassy of Mauritius, 4301 Connecticut Avenue, NW, Suite 134, Washington, D.C. 20008)

"Rhodesia, A House Divided." *National Geographic,* May, 1975.

INDEX